FACTS
CRAZIER
THAN FICTION

Published by Willow Creek Press, Inc.
P.O. Box 147, Minocqua, Wisconsin 54548

Printed in the United States

FACTS
CRAZIER
THAN FICTION

WILLOW CREEK PRESS

SMOKEY BEAR HAS HIS OWN ZIP CODE.

Due to the large volume of mail addressed to him, the United States Postal Service assigned Smokey Bear his own ZIP code, 20252, in 1964. This unique ZIP code was created to handle the flood of letters from children and others concerned about preventing forest fires and preserving the environment.

ULYSSES S. GRANT WAS GIVEN A SPEEDING TICKET WHILE HE WAS PRESIDENT.

Ulysses S. Grant was known to enjoy riding his horse and carriage at high speeds through the streets of Washington, D.C. On at least one occasion, he was stopped by a police officer for speeding. According to historical accounts, he was fined for his fast driving.

THE LONGEST NOODLE EVER MADE MEASURED ALMOST 2 MILES IN LENGTH.

"BUFFALO BUFFALO BUFFALO BUFFALO BUFFALO BUFFALO BUFFALO BUFFALO" IS A GRAMMATICALLY CORRECT SENTENCE.

SATURN'S RINGS ARE MADE FROM TRILLIONS OF CHUNKS OF ORBITING ICE.

IF YOU OPEN YOUR EYES IN A PITCH-BLACK ROOM, THE COLOR YOU'LL SEE IS CALLED "EIGENGRAU."

Eigengrau is a very faint shade of gray that is seen when there is absolutely no light present. It is the color of the human eye's natural adaptation to darkness. It is not a color that can be seen in the presence of any light source but only in complete darkness.

FINGER-PULLING IS AN AUSTRIAN SPORT.

THE FIRST FOOD CONSUMED ON THE MOON WAS COMMUNION BREAD AND WINE.

PARTS OF THE GREAT WALL OF CHINA WERE MADE WITH STICKY RICE.

NASA MISTAKENLY SOLD THE ORIGINAL TAPES OF THE FIRST STEPS ON THE MOON TO AN INTERN FOR $218.

In 1976, the space agency unknowingly sold those tapes of original footage from the Apollo 11 lunar mission to a lucky intern who held onto them for decades. He never even knew their contents.

A WOODPECKER'S TONGUE WRAPS AROUND ITS BRAIN.

THE INVENTOR OF THE WEB ROTARY PRESS WAS KILLED BY HIS OWN INVENTION.

THE HAWAIIAN ALPHABET HAS ONLY 12 LETTERS.

COWS HAVE BEST FRIENDS AND CAN BECOME STRESSED WHEN THEY ARE SEPARATED FROM THEM.

THERE ARE WHALES ALIVE WHO ARE OLDER THAN THE BOOK "MOBY DICK."

TIFFANY & CO. WAS FOUNDED
BEFORE
THE COUNTRY OF ITALY.

In 1837, Charles Lewis Tiffany and John B. Young established Tiffany & Young. The company was rebranded as Tiffany & Co. in 1853. Meanwhile, in 1861, years after its founding and while in Rome, General Giuseppe Garibaldi spearheaded a victorious effort to unify the diverse city-states that now form the country of Italy, consolidating them into a single nation as we recognize it today.

BEAVERS WERE ONCE THE SIZE OF BEARS.

Millions of years ago, giant beavers roamed what is now called Minnesota. More than twice as heavy as modern beavers, the 200-pound mammals had long teeth and powerful jaws. The megafauna were about the size of a modern black bear.

THERE'S ENOUGH CONCRETE IN THE HOOVER DAM TO BUILD A TWO-LANE HIGHWAY FROM SAN FRANCISCO TO NEW YORK CITY.

STEVEN SPIELBERG HAS BEEN THANKED MORE TIMES THAN GOD IN THE ACADEMY AWARDS.

The filmmaker has been mentioned forty-two times whereas people thanked God only nineteen times.

A TIGER'S ROAR CAN BE HEARD UP TO TWO MILES AWAY.

Why are a tiger's pipes so powerful? It turns out they can stretch their vocal cords in a special way that pumps up the volume of their vocalizations.

IF NASA SENT BIRDS INTO SPACE THEY WOULD SOON DIE. THEY NEED GRAVITY TO SWALLOW.

IN ANCIENT EGYPT, THE WORD FOR "CAT" WAS ACTUALLY PRONOUNCED "MEW," OR "MEOW."

ANCIENT ROMANS USED URINE AS MOUTHWASH.

PIGS CAN RUN A SEVEN—MINUTE MILE.

THE CURRENT U.S. FLAG WAS DESIGNED BY A 17-YEAR-OLD FOR A SCHOOL PROJECT. HE GOT A B-.

IN 18TH CENTURY ENGLAND, GAMBLING DENS EMPLOYED SOMEONE WHOSE JOB WAS TO SWALLOW THE DICE IF THERE WAS A POLICE RAID.

COCA–COLA IS OLDER THAN THE EIFFEL TOWER.

THE FIRST RECORDED SWIMMING RACES WERE HELD IN JAPAN IN 36 BC.

QUEEN ELIZABETH II HAD A BODY DOUBLE.

Up until the death of Queen Elizabeth II in September 2022, Ella Slack acted as the late monarch's stand-in, but only in very specific situations. Pensioner Slack didn't particularly resemble the former queen, but was chosen as her "double" as she is of a similar height and build.

PORTLAND, OREGON, WAS NAMED IN A COIN TOSS.

The City of Portland's two founders, Francis Pettygrove from Portland, Maine and Asa Lovejoy from Boston, Massachusetts, both wanted to name the fledgling site, known as The Clearing, after their respective home towns. The coin toss was decided in 1845 with two out of three tosses which Pettygrove won.

THERE ARE DIFFERENT SIZES OF INFINITY.

THE
MONA LISA
HAS NO EYEBROWS.

Some art historians believe that the lack of these features may have been a deliberate choice by Leonardo da Vinci, the artist behind the painting, as it was a common style during the Renaissance to depict women with subtly defined facial features. Another theory suggests that the eyebrows and eyelashes may have faded or been accidentally removed during restoration efforts over the centuries. Ultimately, the exact reason remains a subject of debate among art experts.

GEORGE WASHINGTON
NEVER KNEW
DINOSAURS EXISTED.

Today, the existence of dinosaurs may seem like an immutable fact, but our knowledge of these ancient creatures is a relatively modern development. In fact, the very concept of dinosaurs is so recent that many of the founders of the United States lived most if not all of their lives without knowing that dinos existed.

THE PRINTING PRESS, WHICH REVOLUTIONIZED THE SHARING OF INFORMATION, WAS INVENTED BY GUTENBERG AROUND THE YEAR 1440.

THE FIRST EVER OLYMPIC GAME WAS WON BY A CHEF.

The first Olympic champion listed in the records was Coroebus of Elis, a cook, who won the sprint race in 776 BC.

BOANTHROPY IS THE PSYCHOLOGICAL DISORDER IN WHICH PATIENTS BELIEVE THEY ARE A COW.

THE HOTTEST CHILI PEPPER IN THE WORLD IS THE PEPPER X.

On August 23, 2023, Guinness World Records officially recognized Pepper X as the world's hottest chili pepper, measuring 2.69 million SHU.

AUSTRALIA EXPORTS SAND TO SAUDI ARABIA.

EUKONKANTO IS A WIFE-CARRYING CONTEST.

THE U.S. GOVERNMENT ONCE RENTED CAVES IN MISSOURI TO STORE ITS EXCESS CHEESE.

Hundreds of feet below the ground in Missouri, there are hundreds of thousands of pounds of American cheese. Deep in converted limestone mines, caves kept perfectly at 36 degrees Fahrenheit store stockpiles of government-owned cheese comprising the country's 1.4 billion pounds of surplus cheese.

MORE THAN 80 PERCENT OF THE EARTH'S OCEAN IS UNMAPPED, UNOBSERVED, AND UNEXPLORED.

HYPNOTISM IS BANNED BY PUBLIC SCHOOLS IN SAN DIEGO.

THE PLATYPUS IS ONE OF THE FEW MAMMALS TO PRODUCE VENOM.

The venom is made in venom glands that are connected to hollow spurs on their hind legs; it is primarily made during the mating season. While the venom's effects are described as extremely painful, it is not lethal to humans.

IN AN AIRPLANE, A TRIP TO PLUTO WOULD TAKE ABOUT 800 YEARS.

SPAIN BUILDS HUMAN TOWERS AS PART OF A TRADITIONAL CELEBRATION CALLED "CASTELLS."

ORCAS ARE A NATURAL PREDATOR TO MOOSE.

TIME STOPS

AT THE SPEED OF LIGHT.

When you reach the speed of light, in order for the light to maintain its speed, time would stop as it takes an infinite amount of time for light to reach 300 million meters.

CHILDREN GROW
FASTER
IN THE SPRINGTIME.

Children tend to grow faster in the spring and summer due to a combination of factors. During these seasons, there is more daylight, which can lead to increased physical activity and outdoor play. This, in turn, can stimulate growth and development. Additionally, the abundance of fresh fruits and vegetables during these seasons can provide essential nutrients that support healthy growth. The warmer weather may also contribute to better overall health, which can positively impact a child's growth.

A FULL HEAD OF HUMAN HAIR IS STRONG ENOUGH TO SUPPORT UP TO 12 TONS IN WEIGHT.

Human hair is made of keratin, a powerful structural protein found in horse hooves, animal claws, and our outer layer of skin. Keratin's cross-linking nature allows for hair's unbelievable tensile strength.

POSSUMS DO NOT PLAY DEAD. THEY PASS OUT FROM FEAR OF THEIR PREDATORS.

THE SMALLEST BONE IN YOUR BODY IS IN YOUR EAR.

BACK TO THE FUTURE WAS ALMOST CALLED SPACEMAN FROM PLUTO.

Universal Pictures head Sid Sheinberg apparently didn't like the original title, saying no one would see a movie with the word "future" in the title.

HUMAN BLOOD CELLS HAVE DIFFERENT LIFESPANS.

THERE ARE 19 DIFFERENT ANIMAL SHAPES IN THE ANIMAL CRACKER ZOO.

GIRAFFES HAVE NO VOCAL CORDS.

ICE CREAM WAS ONCE CALLED "CREAM ICE."

CAR MANUFACTURER VOLKSWAGEN MAKES SAUSAGES.

WILLIAM HOWARD TAFT WAS THE LAST U.S. PRESIDENT WITH FACIAL HAIR.

THE LONGEST RECORDED FLIGHT OF A CHICKEN IS 13 SECONDS.

The longest recorded flight of a modern chicken lasted 13 seconds for a distance of just over three hundred feet. It may not sound like much, but for those wrangling a flock of backyard chickens, fifty feet may be all the distance it takes to encounter unhappy neighbors, angry dogs or busy roads.

THE SMALLEST PARK IN THE WORLD IS A CIRCLE IN A STREET TWO FEET ACROSS.

Mill Ends Park is a tiny urban park, consisting of one tree, located in the median strip of SW Naito Parkway in downtown Portland, Oregon. The park is a small circle two feet across, with a total area of 452 square inches.

THERE ARE ONLY TWO COUNTRIES IN THE WORLD THAT USE THE COLOR PURPLE IN THEIR FLAG.

GARLIC IS KNOWN TO ATTRACT LEECHES.

ANCIENT EGYPTIANS SLEPT ON PILLOWS MADE OF STONE.

MONGOLIA IS THE LEAST DENSELY POPULATED COUNTRY ON EARTH.

PRAIRIE DOGS
SAY HELLO
WITH KISSES.

Prairie dogs kiss each other as both a form of greeting and a way to recognize each other. They even kiss their enemies.

MUMMIES CAN
STILL HAVE
FINGERPRINTS.

Fingerprints are one of the few parts of the human body that generally never change—in some cases, even after thousands of years. Scientists who study ancient civilizations by way of mummified remains can attest that mummies have fingerprints.

PEANUTS AREN'T NUTS; THEY'RE LEGUMES.

Peanuts are legumes, which are edible seeds enclosed in pods and are in the same family as beans, lentils and peas.

MARTIN LUTHER KING, JR., ANNE FRANK, AND BARBARA WALTERS WERE BORN IN THE SAME YEAR.

FISH COUGH.

EVERY PERSON HAS A UNIQUE TONGUE PRINT.

THE FAX MACHINE WAS INVENTED WHILE PEOPLE WERE STILL TRAVELING ON THE OREGON TRAIL.

SYLVESTER STALLONE WROTE THE FIRST DRAFT OF ROCKY IN JUST THREE DAYS.

DUELING WAS LEGAL IN URUGUAY UNTIL 1992.

The last official duel took place in 1971 between two politicians after one was called a coward. Another came close in 1990 between a police inspector and newspaper editor, but the inspector backed down. It has since been made forbidden in 1992.

THE CAT IN "THE GODFATHER" OPENING SCENE WAS A STRAY.

IN 1841, CONNECTICUT BANNED NINE-PIN BOWLING TO STOP GAMBLING, LEADING TO THE INVENTION OF TEN-PIN BOWLING TO CIRCUMVENT THE LAW.

THERE ARE ONLY TWO COUNTRIES IN THE WORLD THAT HAVE "THE" AS PART OF THEIR COUNTRY'S NAME.

Countries like Ukraine have dismissed the use of "the Ukraine" in reference to the country. Others such as The Gambia have formally incorporated the article "the" in their name. According to the U.S. Department of State and other authoritative sources, only The Gambia and The Bahamas should formally include the article.

IN ENGLAND, THE SPEAKER OF THE HOUSE IS NOT ALLOWED TO SPEAK.

FIREFIGHTERS SOMETIMES USE WETTING AGENTS TO MAKE WATER WETTER.

In the mid-1960s, fire brigades began to use wetting agents in order to make the water "wetter." The chemical agents are liquid concentrates which, when added to plain water in proper quantities, materially reduce the surface tension of plain water and increase its penetration and spreading ability.

IF THE SUN DIES, IT'LL TAKE ABOUT EIGHT MINUTES BEFORE WE REALIZE IT HAS.

"DREAMT" IS THE ONLY ENGLISH WORD THAT ENDS IN THE LETTERS "MT."

SPAIN AND BOSNIA AND HERZEGOVINA HAVE NATIONAL ANTHEMS WITHOUT OFFICIAL LYRICS.

BIRDS
DON'T
URINATE.

Birds do not release urine from the body through an opening at the end of a urethra. Once the urine passes through the ureters to reach the cloacal chambers, the urine and feces mix together and leave the bird's body through the cloacal opening.

HARVARD WAS FOUNDED BEFORE THE INVENTION OF CALCULUS.

Established in 1636, Harvard is the oldest institution of higher education in the U.S. The "New College," as it was originally called, had no calculus classes because it didn't exist yet.

THE LIBRARY OF CONGRESS CONTAINS APPROXIMATELY 838 MILES OF BOOKSHELVES, LONG ENOUGH TO STRETCH FROM HOUSTON TO CHICAGO.

IT COSTS MORE TO BUY A NEW CAR TODAY IN THE UNITED STATES THAN IT COST CHRISTOPHER COLUMBUS TO EQUIP AND UNDERTAKE THREE VOYAGES TO AND FROM THE NEW WORLD.

WARREN HARDING BET WHITE HOUSE CHINA ON A POKER GAME.

SNICKERS CANDY BAR WAS NAMED AFTER ONE OF FRANK MARS' FAVORITE HORSES.

BLUEBERRY JELLY BELLIES WERE CREATED ESPECIALLY FOR RONALD REAGAN.

THE MOST LAYERS IN A SANDWICH IS 60.

The Di Lusso Deli Company in New York set the Guinness World Record for the "most layers in a sandwich" by making a 60-layer sandwich. The mustard and salami sandwich had to stand on its own for a minute to set the record.

THE TOUR DE FRANCE HAS BEEN HELD ANNUALLY SINCE 1903, EXCEPT DURING THE TWO WORLD WARS.

THE SKELETONS USED IN THE SWIMMING POOL SCENE OF "POLTERGEIST" WERE REAL.

POTATOES WERE BANNED IN FRANCE BECAUSE IT WAS BELIEVED THEY CAUSED LEPROSY.

In 1748 the French Parliament forbade the cultivation of the potato on the grounds that it was thought to cause leprosy. This law remained in effect until 1772.

IN WWII BRITISH SOLDIERS HAD TO MAKE DO WITH ONLY THREE SHEETS OF TOILET PAPER PER DAY.

A TOWN IN PENNSYLVANIA HAS HAD AN UNCONTROLLED FIRE BURNING SINCE 1962.

Centralia, Pennsylvania, is a former mining community located about two hours northwest of Philadelphia in Columbia County. Since 1962, an underground coal fire has been smoldering right below the town.

ALMOST 50 PIGS PLAYED BABE.

JAPAN IS MADE UP OF 6,852 ISLANDS.

THE LONGEST GOLF HOLE IN THE WORLD IS THE 7TH HOLE OF THE SANO COURSE AT SATSUKI GOLF CLUB IN JAPAN, MEASURING 909 YARDS.

BELARUS IS KNOWN AS THE "LUNGS OF EUROPE" DUE TO ITS EXTENSIVE FORESTS.

SOMEONE PAID
$10,000
FOR INVISIBLE ARTWORK.

An art collector once paid $10,000 for a "non-visible" sculpture created by actor James Franco. The artwork was billed as an "endless tank of oxygen."

MAINE IS THE CLOSEST STATE TO AFRICA.

Not only is northern Maine closest to Africa but there's a theory that the mountains that run through it, the Appalachian Mountains, used to be part of the mountains that extend though western Morocco, the Anti-Atlas Mountains in the northwest of Africa.

THE DINGO FENCE IN AUSTRALIA IS LONGER THAN THE DISTANCE BETWEEN NEW YORK CITY AND LONDON.

As one of the longest structures in the world, the dingo fence is an Australian landmark. It stretches more than 3,480 miles across three states, including 93 miles that traverses the red sand dunes of the Strzelecki Desert.

A COSTA RICAN WORKER WHO MAKES BASEBALLS EARNS ABOUT $2,750 ANNUALLY. THE AVERAGE AMERICAN PRO BASEBALL PLAYER EARNS $2,377,000 PER YEAR.

EATING BANANAS CAN HELP FIGHT DEPRESSION BECAUSE THEY CONTAIN THE MOOD-REGULATING SUBSTANCE TRYPTOPHAN.

THE WORLD'S OLDEST CHOCOLATE BAR IS OVER 100 YEARS OLD.

CLEO AND CAESAR WERE THE EARLY STAGE NAMES OF CHER AND SONNY BONO.

YOU GET GOOSEBUMPS WHEN YOU'RE SCARED TO MAKE YOURSELF LOOK BIGGER.

The pilomotor reflex in animals often has the effect of making an animal look bigger. This might help to scare away potential enemies that may have caused the fear reaction in the first place.

HUMANS ARE THE ONLY ANIMALS WITH CHINS.

BULLET PROOF VESTS, FIRE ESCAPES, WINDSHIELD WIPERS AND LASER PRINTERS WERE ALL INVENTED BY WOMEN.

THE ICONIC VOICE OF E.T. WAS PRODUCED BY A WOMAN.

The film's sound designer overheard a woman in a camera store and knew she had just the right pitch. Her name was Pat Walsh, a Californian housewife who smoked a reported two packs of cigarettes a day, giving her voice that recognizable raspy tone.

A GROUP OF OWLS IS CALLED A PARLIAMENT.

MONACO IS SMALLER THAN CENTRAL PARK IN NEW YORK CITY.

At only 0.78 square miles, Monaco is smaller than New York's Central Park. It's second only in size to the Vatican City, but it also holds the distinction of being the world's most densely populated country. It is estimated that you could walk across the entire width of the country in less than an hour.

ONE OF THE WORLD'S OLDEST PRESERVED MEALS IS A 2,400-YEAR-OLD BOWL OF NOODLES FOUND IN CHINA.

CAMEL'S MILK DOES NOT CURDLE.

A "MOMENT" TECHNICALLY LASTS 90 SECONDS.

SAFFRON IS MORE
EXPENSIVE
THAN GOLD BY WEIGHT.

Saffron can only be harvested and processed by hand as its petals must be peeled away gently to collect the delicate saffron threads. Consequently, an ounce of saffron is valued at more than an ounce of gold.

RATS
LAUGH
WHEN TICKLED.

When you tickle rats, they laugh. Their voices are so high-pitched that you need special equipment to hear them, but once you do, you can hear their laughter right away.

MOST OF "THE BLAIR WITCH PROJECT" WAS IMPROVISED AND THE ACTORS GENUINELY BELIEVED THEY WERE PART OF A DOCUMENTARY.

THE FIRST NATIVE AMERICANS TO HELP THE PILGRIMS, NAMED SAMOSET AND TISQUANTUM "SQUANTO" COULD BOTH SPEAK ENGLISH BEFORE HAVING MET THE SETTLERS.

Tisquantum, known commonly as Squanto, spoke fluent English after he was kidnapped and taken to Europe. He lived with the Pilgrims.

WILT CHAMBERLAIN SCORED 100 POINTS IN A SINGLE NBA GAME, THE HIGHEST BY A PLAYER IN A SINGLE GAME.

ANTS TAKE REST FOR AROUND EIGHT MINUTES IN 12-HOUR PERIOD.

THE TWIST TIE COLOR ON BREAD PACKAGING INDICATES THE DAY THE BREAD WAS BAKED.

These color-coded tags indicate the date the bread was baked and packaged. It helps staff keep track of what was baked when, so they can rotate out older loaves as needed.

DONALD DUCK COMICS WERE BANNED IN FINLAND BECAUSE HE DOESN'T WEAR PANTS.

MAY 29 IS OFFICIALLY "PUT A PILLOW ON YOUR FRIDGE DAY."

IF BETELGEUSE EXPLODED RIGHT NOW, THE STAR'S LAST LIGHT SHOW WOULD BRIGHTEN OUR SKY FOR AROUND TWO MONTHS.

THERE'S A BASKETBALL COURT ABOVE THE SUPREME COURT. IT'S KNOWN AS THE HIGHEST COURT IN THE LAND.

PUMBAA WAS THE FIRST DISNEY CHARACTER TO FART.

KFC FOLLOWS 11 PEOPLE ON TWITTER.

Kentucky Fried Chicken follows six men named Herb and the five Spice Girls, from the all-girl British pop group, in what appears to be a nod to the company's original-recipe blend of 11 herbs and spices.

THE MANTIS SHRIMP HAS THE WORLD'S FASTEST PUNCH, MOVING AS FAST AS A BULLET.

The generally accepted analogy of the potency or power behind a mantis shrimp strike is that it has about the same impact power of a typical .22 caliber bullet and their chitinous chelipeds deform less than a lead bullet, so they can do as much or more damage. Some have even broken the glass of their aquariums.

YOUR BONES ARE STRONGER THAN STEEL, OUNCE FOR OUNCE.

BEING ON TIME
IS RUDE
IN VENEZUELA.

It is customary to arrive at least 15 minutes later than the scheduled time, and arriving on time can even be seen as rude or impolite. This cultural norm is known as "la hora venezolana" or "Venezuelan time," and it is deeply ingrained in the country's social fabric.

JUPITER
HAS OVER
90 MOONS.

There are 95 moons of Jupiter with confirmed orbits as of 2024. This number does not include a number of meter-sized moonlets thought to be shed from the inner moons, nor hundreds of possible kilometer-sized outer irregular moons that were only briefly captured by telescopes.

FLUTES MADE FROM A BIRD BONE, OVER 40,000 YEARS OLD, WERE FOUND IN GERMANY.

Scientists unearthed the instruments at Geissenklösterle Cave in Germany, and used carbon dating to find that the flutes are between 42,000 and 43,000 years old, tracing back to the Aurignacian culture from the upper Paleolithic period.

THE OLDEST PERSON ON EARTH WAS BORN CLOSER TO THE SIGNING OF THE UNITED STATES CONSTITUTION THAN TO TODAY.

IF YOU LIFT A KANGAROO'S TAIL OFF THE GROUND, IT CAN'T HOP.

HALF OF ALL HUMANS WHO HAVE EVER LIVED HAVE DIED FROM MALARIA.

DURING YOUR LIFETIME, YOU WILL PRODUCE ENOUGH SALIVA TO FILL 50 BATHTUBS.

JUPITER'S GREAT RED SPOT IS A STORM THAT HAS BEEN RAGING FOR OVER 150 YEARS.

Located in Jupiter's Southern Hemisphere, it is the largest storm in our solar system, appearing as a giant red spot on Jupiter's surface. It has existed for the last 150 years, possibly even longer.

BANANAS ARE CURVED BECAUSE THEY GROW TOWARDS THE SUN.

"JAWS" WAS THE FIRST FILM TO REACH THE $100 MILLION MARK AT THE BOX OFFICE, CREATING THE CONCEPT OF THE "BLOCKBUSTER."

THE DANCING PLAGUE OF 1518 WAS A CASE OF DANCING MANIA THAT OCCURRED IN GERMANY, WHERE PEOPLE DANCED WITHOUT REST FOR A MONTH STRAIGHT.

In July 1518, a woman whose name was given as Frau Troffea stepped into the street and began dancing. She seemed unable to stop and she kept dancing until she collapsed from exhaustion. After resting, she resumed the compulsive frenzied activity. She continued this way for days, and within a week as many as 400 people were eventually consumed by the dancing compulsion. A number of them died from their exertions.

A SQUID'S BRAIN IS SHAPED LIKE A DONUT.

BIRD DROPPINGS ARE THE CHIEF EXPORT OF NAURU, AN ISLAND NATION IN THE WESTERN PACIFIC.

THE POPULATION OF IRELAND IS STILL TWO MILLION LESS THAN IT WAS BEFORE THE POTATO FAMINE, 160 YEARS AGO.

CHEROPHOBIA IS THE IRRATIONAL FEAR OF FUN OR HAPPINESS.

TOMATOES WERE ONCE BELIEVED TO BE POISONOUS.

In the late 1700s, Europeans drew a false connection to dying aristocrats. These ill-fated aristocrats ate tomatoes off pewter plates and often got sick and died after ingesting the red fruit. But the cause of death was actually due to the high lead content of their pewter plates.

PIGEONS CAN DO MATH AS WELL AS MONKEYS.

Scientists have found that pigeons are much smarter than we give them credit for and can be taught some complex abstract math. This is stunning because it's a trait that has only been shown in primates. But according to a report in the journal Science, researchers were able to teach pigeons abstract rules about math.

GLACIERS, ICE CAPS, AND ICE SHEETS HOLD NEARLY 69 PERCENT OF THE WORLD'S FRESHWATER.

If all land ice melted the seas would rise about 230 feet. During the last ice age (when glaciers covered more land area than today) the sea level was about 400 feet lower than it is today.

THE HUM OF THE LIGHTSABERS IN STAR WARS WAS CREATED BY COMBINING THE SOUND OF AN OLD MOVIE PROJECTOR AND THE BUZZ FROM A TELEVISION SET.

BATS ALWAYS TURN LEFT WHEN EXITING A CAVE.

A CORNED BEEF SANDWICH WAS SMUGGLED INTO SPACE ON THE GEMINI 3 MISSION IN 1965.

As contraband unapproved for flight by NASA, pilot John Young had hidden the sandwich in a pocket of his spacesuit shortly before the launch.

HART ISLAND IS THE FINAL BURIAL PLACE FOR OVER A MILLION OF NEW YORK CITY'S UNCLAIMED BODIES.

THE INVENTOR OF VASELINE USED TO EAT IT.

SAINT LUCIA IS THE ONLY COUNTRY IN THE WORLD NAMED AFTER A WOMAN.

THE BATTLE OF HASTINGS DIDN'T ACTUALLY TAKE PLACE IN HASTINGS.

It actually took place in a field seven miles from Hastings. That spot grew, after being founded as the commemorative Battle Abbey in 1095, into the appropriately named town of Battle.

THE MICHELIN STAR RATING FOR RESTAURANTS ORIGINALLY STARTED AS A WAY TO ENCOURAGE MORE ROAD TRAVEL, TIRE USAGE, AND THUS TIRE PURCHASES.

ABBA TURNED DOWN ONE BILLION DOLLARS TO DO A REUNION TOUR.

BANK ROBBER JOHN DILLINGER PLAYED PROFESSIONAL BASEBALL.

DIRECTOR ALFRED HITCHCOCK MADE A BRIEF APPEARANCE IN ALMOST ALL OF HIS FILMS.

The majority of his appearances occur within the first half-hour of his films, with over half in the first 15 minutes. Hitchcock's longest cameo appearances are in his British films Blackmail and Young and Innocent.

THERE ARE A TOTAL OF 1,710 STEPS IN THE EIFFEL TOWER.

HUMANS ARE THE ONLY SPECIES KNOWN TO BLUSH.

AUSTRALIA IS THE ONLY COUNTRY THAT IS ALSO A CONTINENT.

Australia is the only country in the world that covers an entire continent. It is one of the largest countries on Earth. Although it is rich in natural resources and has a lot of fertile land, more than one-third of Australia is desert.

NEIL ARMSTRONG HAD TO GO
THROUGH
CUSTOMS AFTER RETURNING
FROM THE MOON.

After landing back on Earth, the Apollo 11 crew had to go through customs—as though they were returning from another country rather than from space. The items they declared included Moon dust and Moon rocks.

ROD STEWART HOLDS THE RECORD FOR THE LARGEST FREE ROCK CONCERT ATTENDANCE, PERFORMING FOR 3.5 MILLION PEOPLE IN RIO DE JANEIRO ON NEW YEAR'S EVE 1994.

POTATO CHIPS WERE INVENTED BY A CHEF WHO WAS ANNOYED AT A CUSTOMER WHO KEPT SENDING HIS FRIED POTATOES BACK, CLAIMING THEY WERE TOO THICK AND SOGGY.

Legend says chef George Crum became agitated when a customer sent his French-fried potatoes back to the kitchen, complaining that they were cut too thickly. Crum reacted by slicing the potatoes as thin as he possibly could, frying them in grease, and sending the crunchy brown chips back out on the guest's plate that way.

AMERICA ONCE ISSUED A 5-CENT BILL.

THE AVERAGE AMERICAN WILL EAT 35,000 COOKIES IN THEIR LIFETIME.

GIRAFFES HAVE BLACK TONGUES TO PREVENT SUNBURN.

POUND CAKE GOT ITS NAME BECAUSE THE ORIGINAL RECIPE CONTAINED A POUND OF BUTTER, SUGAR, FLOUR, AND EGGS.

ONE IN EVERY 200 PEOPLE HAS AN EXTRA RIB.

"PIRATES OF THE CARIBBEAN: ON STRANGER TIDES" HOLDS THE RECORD FOR THE MOST EXPENSIVE MOVIE EVER MADE, WITH AN ESTIMATED BUDGET OF $379 MILLION.

THE LONGEST ENGLISH WORD IS 189,819 LETTERS LONG. IT'S THE CHEMICAL NAME FOR THE PROTEIN KNOWN AS TITIN.

Methionylthreonylthreonylglutaminylarginyl… isoleucine is the chemical name for the protein of "titin" also known as "connectin." The largest known protein that consists of 26,926 amino acids is made up of 189,819 letters and can take about three hours to pronounce.

FRIDA KAHLO CREATED 143 PAINTINGS. OF THESE, 55 WERE SELF-PORTRAITS.

AN ANIMAL EPIDEMIC IS CALLED AN EPIZOOTIC.

FACEBOOK ENGINEERS ORIGINALLY WANTED TO CALL THE "LIKE" BUTTON THE "AWESOME" BUTTON.

POLAND HAS A FOREST FULL OF CROOKED TREES, KNOWN AS THE CROOKED FOREST.

THE INVENTOR OF THE MICROWAVE APPLIANCE ONLY RECEIVED A $2 BONUS FOR HIS DISCOVERY.

THE FIRST FORD CARS HAD
ENGINES
MADE BY DODGE.

Dodge Brothers, Horace and John, owned a Detroit machine shop and were the source of most Ford-designed engines for several years. At that time they were also stockholders in Ford.

SQUARE WATERMELONS ARE GROWN IN JAPAN.

Known as Shikaku suika in Japanese, these square watermelons were developed in the 1970s by an artist named Tomoyuki Ono. Part of the goal in making these watermelons wasn't only aesthetic but practical. Not only are they easier to pack and ship to market, but they are also conveniently shaped to fit in your refrigerator. Plus, as you'd imagine, they are way easier to cut than a slippery round watermelon.

THE "HURRIAN HYMN NO. 6" IS CONSIDERED THE WORLD'S OLDEST KNOWN MELODY, DATED TO APPROXIMATELY 1400 BC.

THE WORD "SALARY" COMES FROM "SAL," MEANING "SALT" IN LATIN. ROMAN SOLDIERS WERE SOMETIMES PAID IN SALT, HENCE "SALARY."

AFRICAN ELEPHANTS HAVE THE LONGEST PREGNANCY OF ALL THE LAND MAMMALS, NEARLY 22 MONTHS.

THE FILM "LITTLE SHOP OF HORRORS" WAS SHOT IN JUST TWO DAYS.

The Little Shop of Horrors was shot on a budget of $22,500 to $28,000. Interiors were shot in two days, by utilizing sets that had been left standing from "A Bucket of Blood."

ALLIGATORS WILL GIVE MANATEES THE RIGHT OF WAY IF THEY ARE SWIMMING NEAR EACH OTHER.

JUDGE JUDY MAKES $45 MILLION PER YEAR.

THERE ARE SOME SPIDERS THAT KEEP TINY FROGS AS PETS TO STOP PESTS THAT TRY TO EAT THE SPIDER'S EGGS.

This tiny little amphibian finds refuge in the humid burrow which the tarantula protects fiercely. In exchange, the frog eats bugs that threaten her eggs!

PRESIDENT JIMMY CARTER HAD SOLAR PANELS INSTALLED ON THE WHITE HOUSE, BUT HIS SUCCESSOR, PRESIDENT RONALD REAGAN, HAD THEM REMOVED.

MAILMEN IN RUSSIA NOW CARRY REVOLVERS AFTER A RECENT DECISION BY THE GOVERNMENT.

ONE TEASPOON OF NEUTRON STAR MATERIAL WEIGHS SIX BILLION TONS.

NORWAY HAS A 25-YEAR-OLD KING PENGUIN NAMED BRIGADIER SIR NILS OLAV AS A KNIGHT.

DAIRY COWS HAVE BEEN SHOWN TO PRODUCE MORE MILK WHEN LISTENING TO SOOTHING MUSIC.

THE LONGEST BOXING MATCH WENT 110 ROUNDS AND LASTED OVER 7 HOURS.

LEMURS USE
MILLIPEDES
TO GET HIGH.

After the lemur bites the millipede, it sprays its toxic secretion, which the lemur then rubs all over its fur. Research suggests that there is a practical purpose to this: the benzoquinone secretion functions as a natural pesticide and wards off malaria-carrying mosquitoes. The secretion also acts as a narcotic, which causes the lemur to salivate profusely and enter a state of intoxication.

PENGUINS PROPOSE BY GIVING THEIR MATE A PEBBLE.

Gentoo penguins know a good pebble when they see one. Scooping them up in their beaks, they carry them to their partner; a gift that acknowledges the relationship between the two penguins and helps grow the nest for their budding family.

THE LONGEST CRICKET MATCH TOOK PLACE IN 1939 AND LASTED 14 DAYS, ONLY ENDING BECAUSE ONE OF THE TEAMS HAD TO CATCH THEIR SHIP HOME.

WHEN A PERSON GETS A KIDNEY TRANSPLANT, THEY USUALLY JUST LEAVE THE ORIGINAL KIDNEYS IN THEIR BODY AND PUT THE 3RD KIDNEY IN THE LOWER ABDOMEN.

NEWSWEEK MAGAZINE WAS SOLD BY THE WASHINGTON POST CO. FOR $1 IN 2010.

Newsweek was owned by The Washington Post Co. for five decades before being sold in 2010 to the late stereo magnate Sidney Harman, who bought the magazine for $1 and liabilities. Newsweek was founded in 1933, after the creation of its longtime rival, Time.

THE FIRST KNOWN RECIPE BOOK WAS FROM 1730 BC IN MESOPOTAMIA.

DURING WORLD WAR II THE U.S. CREATED A BOMB THAT USED LIVE BATS.

The bomb consisted of a bomb-shaped casing with over a thousand compartments, each containing a hibernating Mexican free-tailed bat with a small, timed incendiary bomb attached.

MOVIE TRAILERS WERE ORIGINALLY SHOWN AFTER THE MOVIE, WHICH IS WHY THEY'RE CALLED "TRAILERS."

ONLY ABOUT 1 IN 10,000 PEOPLE HAVE PERFECT PITCH, THE ABILITY TO IDENTIFY OR RECREATE A MUSICAL NOTE WITHOUT A REFERENCE TONE.

ACCORDING TO GREEK TRADITIONS, TOSSING CHILDREN'S LOOSE TEETH ONTO A ROOF BRINGS GOOD LUCK.

When children lose teeth in Greece, it is customary to make a wish for strong adult teeth as they throw their lost baby teeth onto the roof.

IN TOKYO, YOU CAN BUY A TOUPEE FOR YOUR DOG.

THERE IS ENOUGH WATER IN LAKE SUPERIOR TO COVER ALL OF NORTH AND SOUTH AMERICA IN ONE FOOT OF LIQUID.

THE FOUNDER OF MATCH.COM, GARY KREMEN, LOST HIS GIRLFRIEND TO ANOTHER MAN SHE MET ON MATCH.COM.

ABRAHAM LINCOLN LOST FIVE SEPARATE ELECTIONS BEFORE HE BECAME PRESIDENT OF THE U.S.

THE PAINTING OF GEORGE WASHINGTON USED FOR THE DOLLAR BILL WAS NEVER FINISHED.

AB NEGATIVE IS THE RAREST BLOOD TYPE.

TENNIS WAS ORIGINALLY
PLAYED
WITH BARE HANDS.

The Medieval form of tennis is termed as real tennis, a game that evolved over three centuries from an earlier ball game played around the 12th century in France that involved hitting a ball with a bare hand and later with a glove.

OXFORD UNIVERSITY
IS OLDER
THAN THE AZTEC EMPIRE.

Oxford University was founded in 1096 AD, making it about 250 years older than the Aztec Empire. Located in Oxford, England, Oxford University is the oldest university in the English-speaking world.

BOB BEAMON'S LONG JUMP RECORD SET AT THE MEXICO OLYMPICS IN 1968 WAS SO FAR THAT THE EXISTING MEASURING EQUIPMENT WAS NOT LONG ENOUGH TO MEASURE IT.

THE HORSE IN THE EMERALD CITY PALACE IN "THE WIZARD OF OZ" WAS COLORED WITH JELL-O CRYSTALS.

BIRDS SING IN THEIR DREAMS.

NEW ZEALAND WAS THE FIRST COUNTRY TO GRANT WOMEN THE RIGHT TO VOTE IN 1893.

MINUS 40 DEGREES CELSIUS IS EXACTLY THE SAME AS MINUS 40 DEGREES FAHRENHEIT.

On 19 September 1893, Governor Lord Glasgow signed a new Electoral Act into law, and New Zealand became the first self-governing country in the world to enshrine in law the right for women to vote in parliamentary elections.

HUMANS ARE THE ONLY ANIMALS THAT CRY WHEN EMOTIONAL.

Tears have evolved to be a communicative signal at close range to tell others that we are vulnerable and in need of assistance.

MCDONALD'S SELLS 75 HAMBURGERS EVERY SECOND OF EVERY DAY.

THE LONGEST CIGAR IN THE WORLD IS AS LONG AS A FOOTBALL FIELD.

SMALLPOX IS THE ONLY INFECTIOUS DISEASE THAT AFFECTS HUMANS TO HAVE BEEN ERADICATED.

The last known natural case was in Somalia in 1977. In 1980 WHO declared smallpox eradicated – the only infectious disease to achieve this distinction. This remains among the most notable and profound public health successes in history.

WRESTLING IS CONSIDERED THE WORLD'S OLDEST SPORT, WITH CAVE PAINTINGS SUGGESTING ITS EXISTENCE OVER 15,000 YEARS AGO.

THE AVERAGE ADULT HUMAN HAS TWO TO NINE POUNDS OF BACTERIA IN HIS OR HER BODY.

THE "VIEUXTEMPS GUARNERI" VIOLIN WAS SOLD FOR OVER $16 MILLION, MAKING IT THE MOST EXPENSIVE MUSICAL INSTRUMENT IN THE WORLD.

ARMADILLOS ARE THE ONLY ANIMAL BESIDES HUMANS THAT CAN GET LEPROSY.

A U.S. TOWN HAD A 3-YEAR-OLD MAYOR.

The town of Dorset, Minnesota, holds a yearly election at the "Taste of Dorset" festival, residents paying $1 to add a name of their choice to a hat, with a random slip being drawn to select a mayor. In August 2012, then three-year-old Robert "Bobby" Tufts became mayor for a one-year term, when his name was drawn.

SEA OTTERS HOLD HANDS WHEN THEY SLEEP SO THEY DON'T DRIFT AWAY FROM EACH OTHER.

WHALE SHARKS HAVE
TEETH
ON THEIR EYEBALLS.

Dermal denticles, also known as placoid scales, are the tiny tough scales that cover sharks and rays. But although they are scales as we think of them, they're also structurally very similar to teeth, and include an inner core of pulp, a middle layer of dentine or bony tissue, and a hard enamel-like coating on top.

CROWS OFTEN HOLD GRUDGES AGAINST SPECIFIC PEOPLE.

Crows can recognize humans, which is remarkable in and of itself, but beyond that, they also know which humans are good humans and bad humans based on their previous experiences with them. Those bad humans they might hold grudges against, while good humans might receive gifts.

THE STATE OF OHIO GIVES OUT DIFFERENT COLORED LICENSE PLATES FOR THOSE WITH A DUI CONVICTION.

One part of the sentence for an Ohio DUI / OVI conviction may be a requirement that you have yellow license plates on your vehicle. Although they are commonly referred to as "party plates," Ohio law calls them "restricted license plates."

IN 1943, THE TEMPERATURE IN SPEARFISH, SOUTH DAKOTA JUMPED 49 DEGREES IN TWO MINUTES.

PIGS ARE CONSIDERED TO BE THE WORLD'S FIFTH-SMARTEST ANIMAL.

WHEN YOU SNAP YOUR FINGER, YOUR FINGER MOVES AT ABOUT 20 MPH.

A FOX USES ITS TAIL TO COMMUNICATE WITH OTHER FOXES.

OCTOPUSES ACTUALLY HAVE SIX ARMS AND TWO LEGS.

YOU CAN'T SNEEZE IN YOUR SLEEP.

Sneezing is a reflex that helps expel pollen, dust, and other irritants from your nasal passages. Your brain prevents reflexes in NREM sleep and muscle movements in REM sleep, so you can't sneeze.

A SWARM OF 20,000 BEES FOLLOWED A CAR FOR TWO DAYS AS THEIR QUEEN WAS TRAPPED INSIDE.

THE HUMAN HEART CREATES ENOUGH PRESSURE WHEN IT PUMPS OUT TO THE BODY TO SQUIRT BLOOD 30 FEET.

THE KINGDOM OF BHUTAN MEASURES PROSPERITY BY GROSS NATIONAL HAPPINESS RATHER THAN GDP.

The concept of GDP plays a secondary role in measuring national well-being, especially after 1972 when GNH was formally introduced to the world. The focus has been on developing GNH and its broader philosophical outreach in a modern world of which Bhutan is increasingly becoming part.

MONACO HAS THE MOST MILLIONAIRES AND BILLIONAIRES PER CAPITA.

IF A STATUE OF A PERSON IN THE PARK ON A HORSE HAS BOTH FRONT LEGS IN THE AIR, THE PERSON DIED IN BATTLE. IF THE HORSE HAS ONE FRONT LEG IN THE AIR, THE PERSON DIED AS A RESULT OF WOUNDS RECEIVED IN BATTLE.

COSMIC LATTE IS THE AVERAGE COLOR OF THE UNIVERSE.

COLOMBIA IS CONSIDERED THE WORLD'S LARGEST PRODUCER OF EMERALDS.

FLEAS CAN JUMP 200 TIMES THEIR BODY LENGTH.

Fleas can jump over 8 inches in length and 5 inches in height. This is almost 200 times their own body size! Some fleas have even been recorded jumping up to 19 inches. How do we know? Scientists have used high speed cameras to capture these giant jumps and measure how far the fleas are able to go. Compared to other insects, fleas are champion jumpers.

MORE PEOPLE HAVE BEEN
KILLED BY
MOLASSES THAN BY COYOTES.

The Great Molasses Flood of 1919 killed 21 people, injured 150 others and flattened buildings. In 1919, a massive storage tank in Boston buckled and gave way, releasing 2.3 million gallons of molasses in a wave that measured nearly as high as a football goalpost. Because the molasses was still several degrees warmer than the cold, winter air, when the tank broke, it chilled as it streamed through the streets and the temperature made the molasses more viscous and more difficult for people to disentangle themselves. Meanwhile, only two fatal coyote attacks have been confirmed in the wild.

THERE ARE ICE CAVES IN ICELAND THAT HAVE HOT SPRINGS.

Iceland is a country with high volcanic and geothermal activity. The glaciers covering volcanoes have volcanic vents or hot springs emitting heat, which creates more meltwater. When the water pours down the glacier moulins, it digs tunnels in the ice.

THE HUMAN BODY CONTAINS ENOUGH FAT TO MAKE SEVEN BARS OF SOAP.

THE SMELL OF FRESHLY-CUT GRASS IS ACTUALLY A PLANT DISTRESS CALL.

The smell of cut grass in recent years has been identified as the plant's way of signalling distress, but new research says the aroma also summons beneficial insects to the rescue.

CANADA'S NATIONAL PARKS ARE FREE FOR KIDS.

MOUNT EVEREST HAS BEEN SUMMITED BY CLIMBERS RANGING FROM AGE 13 TO 80.

THE UNITED STATES NAVY USED XBOX CONTROLLERS FOR THEIR PERISCOPES.

ON AVERAGE, MEN GET BORED OF A SHOPPING TRIP AFTER 26 MINUTES.

THE GUINNESS WORLD RECORD FOR THE MOST
VARIETIES OF CHEESE ON A PIZZA IS 834.

ONLY FEMALE MOSQUITOES BITE.

Only female mosquitoes bite people and animals to get a blood meal. Female mosquitoes need a blood meal to produce eggs. Mosquitoes get infected with germs, such as viruses and parasites, when they bite infected people and animals.

WORCESTERSHIRE SAUCE IS MADE FROM DISSOLVED FISH.

Anchovies are always present in Worcestershire sauce, which is essentially a fermented fish sauce. Fresh anchovies have quite a mild taste but after the fish are processed and packed in oil and salt they develop a strong flavor.

HIGH HEELS WERE ORIGINALLY WORN BY MEN.

A STUDY FOUND THAT ORCAS CAN LEARN TO SPEAK DOLPHIN.

Scientists noticed that killer whales who had spent time with bottlenose dolphins incorporated more clicking and whistles in their vocalizations than other whales, making their "language" a mashup of the two.

TROPICAL STORMS AND HURRICANES STARTED GETTING "NAMED" IN 1953.

IN COOKING, 10 DROPS MAKE A DASH.

SNAKES CAN
PREDICT
EARTHQUAKES.

According to some experts, snakes can detect the seismic waves that precede an earthquake. These waves cause the ground to vibrate and the snakes can feel these vibrations through their skin. Snakes have a special organ in their body called the vestibular system, which helps them balance and orient themselves. This organ is very sensitive to changes in movement and pressure, so when the earth shakes, the snakes know something is up.

THE GREAT WALL OF CHINA WAS COMPLETED TWO YEARS AFTER THE FIRST TELEPHONE CALL.

The Great Wall of China was constructed from the 7th Century BC by the Chu State and completed in 1878 in the Qing Dynasty. The world's first telephone call was made in 1876, by Alexander Graham Bell.

AIRLINES SELL ALL THEIR UNCLAIMED BAGGAGE TO A STORE IN SCOTTSBORO, ALABAMA, THAT RESELLS EVERYTHING.

THERE'S AN ITALIAN WINE THAT'S PRODUCED IN A SUBMERGED VESSEL WITHIN THE SEA TO AGE IT.

The bottles of Thalassitis wine, made from the noble Assyrtiko grape variety, are placed at a depth of 82 feet, inside metal cages. They are left there in the sea for 5 long years.

THE UNITED STATES HAS NO OFFICIAL LANGUAGE AT THE FEDERAL LEVEL.

A CHICKEN NAMED MIKE LIVED FOR 18 MONTHS AFTER ITS HEAD WAS CHOPPED OFF.

RONALD REAGAN WAS OFFERED A ROLE IN BACK TO THE FUTURE III.

It's not every day that the President of the United States makes a cameo in a beloved motion picture franchise, and Back to the Future Part III nearly featured Ronald Reagan in a small, supporting role.

THE MOON GETS HIT BY OVER 6,000 POUNDS OF METEOR MATERIAL PER DAY.

"I AM" IS THE SHORTEST COMPLETE SENTENCE IN THE ENGLISH LANGUAGE.

DOSTOEVSKY WROTE THE GAMBLER TO PAY OFF HIS GAMBLING DEBTS.

IF YOU COULD FOLD A PIECE OF PAPER IN HALF 42 TIMES, IT WOULD REACH THE MOON.

30 folds will get you to space, because your paper will now be 100 km high. 42 folds will get you to the Moon, 81 folds and your paper will be 127,786 light-years, almost as thick as the Andromeda Galaxy. At 103 folds, you will get outside of the observable Universe, which is estimated at 93 billion light-years in diameter.

THERE ARE MORE THAN 70 STREETS IN ATLANTA WITH SOME VARIATION OF THE NAME "PEACHTREE."

LEO FENDER, THE INVENTOR OF THE STRATOCASTER AND THE TELECASTER, COULDN'T PLAY GUITAR.

SWEDEN HAS A SKI-THROUGH MCDONALD'S.

JOHN F. KENNEDY'S ETERNAL FLAME IN ARLINGTON NATIONAL CEMETERY HAS ONLY GONE OUT TWICE SINCE 1963.

THE EIGHTH POWER OF A NUMBER IS A ZENZIZENZIZENZIC.

The first time was less than a month after it had been lit when a child accidentally extinguished it with holy water. Luckily one of the grave workers was a smoker and had a lighter on hand to relight it.

AN OSTRICH'S EYE IS BIGGER THAN ITS BRAIN.

CAMEL WRESTLING IS A
POPULAR
SPORT IN TURKEY.

Camel wrestling is a combative sport wherein two male camels are made to wrestle in response to the mating call of a female camel. This happens in a specially built sand and fenced arena and the camels usually wear colorful gear to protect themselves from each other's bite.

THERE'S A VARIETY OF POTATO CALLED "LA BONNOTTE" THAT CAN COST $320 PER POUND.

Le Bonnotte potatoes are a small, delicate and rare variety of potatoes that are considered a delicacy in France. They are only grown on Île de Noirmoutier, an island off the west coast of France, and can only be planted, fertilized and harvested by hand due to their delicate nature.

KERMIT ROOSEVELT, THEODORE ROOSEVELT'S GRANDSON, OVERTHREW IRAN FOR THE U.S. GOVERNMENT.

THE EARTH HAS A WAISTLINE.

THERE IS A SPECIES OF SPIDER CALLED THE HOBO SPIDER.

INSTALLED IN 1410, THE WORLD'S OLDEST ASTRONOMICAL CLOCK STILL IN OPERATION IS IN PRAGUE.

DWIGHT EISENHOWER NAMED CAMP DAVID AFTER HIS GRANDSON.

A MOUSE CAN FIT THROUGH A HOLE THE SIZE OF A BALLPOINT PEN.

Due to their physical characteristic of having a body that is long, cylindrical and flexible, rodents such as mice or rats or hamsters seem to fit into insanely small holes. In general, mice are able to fit through any hole that their skull is able to fit through.

JEFF BEZOS' FATHER WAS A UNICYCLIST IN A CIRCUS.

HELEN KELLER IS RELATED TO ROBERT E. LEE. HER PATERNAL GRANDMOTHER WAS HIS SECOND COUSIN.

THERE ARE MORE POSSIBLE ITERATIONS OF A GAME OF CHESS THAN THERE ARE ATOMS IN THE KNOWN UNIVERSE.

This is the Shannon Number and represents all of the possible move variations in the game of chess.

A POUND OF HOUSEFLIES CONTAINS MORE PROTEIN THAN A POUND OF BEEF.

AUSTRALIA EXPORTS CAMELS TO THE MIDDLE EAST.

JACK BLACK IS THE SON OF ROCKET SCIENTISTS.

THE WORLD'S LARGEST HULA HOOP MEASURES OVER 17 FEET.

TURRITOPSIS DOHRNII, A JELLYFISH SPECIES, IS CONSIDERED BIOLOGICALLY IMMORTAL.

YOUR SMALL INTESTINE IS ABOUT FOUR TIMES AS LONG AS YOU ARE TALL.

While aging affects most living organisms, the hydrozoan Turritopsis dohrnii is the only species able to rejuvenate repeatedly after sexual reproduction, becoming biologically immortal.

MOST PEOPLE FART AROUND 14 TO 23 TIMES A DAY.

SHARKS LIVED ON
EARTH
BEFORE TREES.

The earliest species that could be classified as "tree" lived around 350 million years ago, in forests where the Sahara desert is now, but sharks have been around for 400 million years.

MOSQUITOES HAVE 47 "TEETH."

Mosquitoes have a six-pronged microneedle system, which allows them to pierce the skin and find blood vessels. Two of their outermost needles have 47 tiny "teeth," which they use to saw through skin. Through the proboscis, the mosquito injects a bit of its saliva as a coagulant.

MONTANA'S GLACIER NATIONAL PARK HAS A CANINE "BARK RANGER" THAT HELPS HERD WILDLIFE AWAY FROM HIGH-TRAFFIC AREAS.

IN 2013, BELGIUM ISSUED LIMITED EDITION CHOCOLATE-FLAVORED POSTAGE STAMPS.

To celebrate Belgium's renowned chocolatiers, the country's post office, Bpost, launched a set of limited-edition stamps that smell and taste like chocolate.

NORTH KOREA AND CUBA ARE THE ONLY PLACES YOU CAN'T BUY COCA-COLA.

COLOGNE WAS ORIGINALLY PRODUCED AS PROTECTION AGAINST THE PLAGUE. IT WAS WIDELY BELIEVED THAT BAD-SMELLING AIR SPREAD THE DISEASE.

YOUR LIVER CAN REGENERATE ITSELF COMPLETELY.

The liver can regenerate after either surgical removal or after chemical injury. It is known that as little as 25% of the original liver mass can regenerate back to its full size. The process of regeneration in mammals is mainly compensatory growth because only the mass of the liver is replaced, not the shape.

THERE'S A RIVER CALLED "BIG UGLY CREEK" IN WEST VIRGINIA.

THE DEAD SEA, LOCATED BETWEEN JORDAN AND ISRAEL, IS THE LOWEST POINT ON EARTH.

IN SPACE, YOU DON'T NEED WELDING MATERIALS TO GET TWO METALS TO FUSE.

If two pieces of the same type of metal touch in space, they will bond and be permanently stuck together. This phenomenon is known as cold welding. or contact welding, and it occurs in the vacuum of space. In this welding method, heat is not the primary element for fusing metals.

THE UNITED KINGDOM HAS INVADED ALL BUT 22 COUNTRIES IN THE WORLD AT SOME POINT IN HISTORY.

"YESTERDAY" BY THE BEATLES IS ONE OF THE MOST COVERED SONGS IN THE HISTORY OF RECORDED MUSIC, WITH OVER 2,200 VERSIONS.

YOU CAN'T KILL YOURSELF BY HOLDING YOUR BREATH.

Scientific consensus is that you can't kill yourself by holding your breath: as soon as you fall unconscious, your autonomous nervous system will take over and you'll resume breathing normally.

A CYBERCHONDRIAC IS SOMEONE WHO SCOURS THE INTERNET LOOKING FOR DETAILS OF THEIR ILLNESSES.

THE WORD "BURRITO" MEANS "LITTLE DONKEY" IN SPANISH.

BOB DYLAN'S BIRTH NAME WAS ROBERT ZIMMERMAN.

LIZARDS COMMUNICATE
BY DOING
PUSH-UPS.

This behavior conveys information about that individual, like how strong and fit they are, as both a warning to potential competitors and to attract potential mates.

A SMALL CHILD COULD SWIM

THROUGH

THE VEINS OF A BLUE WHALE.

Pretty much everything about the blue whale is massive. Its tongue weighs as much as an elephant, its heart is the size of a car and its blood vessels are so wide a small child could swim through them.

NADIA COMANECI WAS THE FIRST GYMNAST TO SCORE A PERFECT 10 AT THE OLYMPICS, IN 1976.

YOUR BODY CONTAINS ABOUT 0.2 MILLIGRAMS OF GOLD, MOST OF IT IN YOUR BLOOD.

It's been found that the element plays an important health function, helping to maintain our joints, as well as facilitating the transmittal of electrical signals throughout the body.

TWINKIES HAVE A SHELF LIFE OF 45 DAYS.

LISTENING TO MUSIC CAN SYNCHRONIZE THE LISTENER'S HEART RATE TO THE RHYTHM OF THE MUSIC.

"CLEOPATRA" WAS SO EXPENSIVE THAT IT NEARLY BANKRUPTED 20TH CENTURY FOX.

CANADA'S FORESTS MAKE UP NEARLY 9% OF THE WORLD'S TOTAL FOREST AREA.

Canada has 9% of the world's forest but is responsible for only 0.37% of global deforestation that has occurred since 1990. The main drivers of deforestation in Canada continue to be agriculture, mining, and oil and gas expansion.

NETFLIX IS RESPONSIBLE FOR 15% OF GLOBAL INTERNET TRAFFIC.

WHITE CHOCOLATE ISN'T TECHNICALLY CHOCOLATE AS IT CONTAINS NO COCOA SOLIDS.

BEFORE HE WAS PRESIDENT, GROVER CLEVELAND WAS A HANGMAN.

THE WORD "Y'ALL" DATES BACK TO AT LEAST 1631.

According to historian David Parker, the earliest occurrence of "y'all" was found in 1631.

FROZEN COW POO WAS THE FIRST-EVER PUCK USED IN A HOCKEY GAME.

YOU CAN VISIT THE "FUTURE BIRTHPLACE" OF STAR TREK'S CAPTAIN KIRK IN RIVERSIDE, IOWA.

UNTIL THE EARLY 19TH CENTURY, AUSTRALIA WAS BEST KNOWN AS "NEW HOLLAND."

IN RUSSIA, BEER WAS CONSIDERED A SOFT DRINK, NOT ALCOHOL, UNTIL 2011.

Beer was legally classified as an alcoholic drink in Russia in 2011, after former Russian President Dmitry Medvedev signed the bill. Until then, anything containing less than 10% alcohol was considered foodstuff in Russia.

54 MILLION PEOPLE ALIVE RIGHT NOW WILL BE DEAD WITHIN 12 MONTHS.

ASKING FOR SALT IN AN
EGYPTIAN
HOUSEHOLD IS CONSIDERED RUDE.

If you ask for salt or pepper in Egypt, you may hurt people's feelings. It's a message to the person who's cooked a dish letting them know that it's not tasty enough and that you need to "complete" their work.

DRINKING TOO MUCH
WATER
CAN BE FATAL.

Water intoxication, also known as water poisoning, hyperhydration, overhydration, water toxemia or hyponatremia is a potentially fatal disturbance in brain functions that can result when the normal balance of electrolytes in the body is pushed outside safe limits by excessive water intake.

BHUTAN IS THE ONLY COUNTRY IN THE WORLD WITH A CARBON NEGATIVE FOOTPRINT.

PEOPLE LIVING IN THE SOUTHERN HEMISPHERE SEE THE MOON UPSIDE DOWN COMPARED TO PEOPLE LIVING IN THE NORTHERN HEMISPHERE.

LIECHTENSTEIN AND UZBEKISTAN ARE THE ONLY TWO DOUBLY LANDLOCKED COUNTRIES IN THE WORLD.

THE WORLD'S OLDEST WOODEN WHEEL HAS BEEN AROUND FOR MORE THAN 5,000 YEARS.

In 2002 Slovenian archaeologists uncovered a wooden wheel some 12 miles southeast of Ljubljana. It was established that the wheel is between 5,100 and 5,350 years old.

R2-D2 WAS SUPPOSED TO SPEAK ENGLISH.

THE COLOR ORANGE WAS ACTUALLY NAMED AFTER ORANGES.

KANSAS PRODUCES ENOUGH WHEAT EACH YEAR TO FEED EVERYONE IN THE WORLD FOR ABOUT TWO WEEKS.

THE FASTEST A DOLPHIN CAN SWIM NEAR THE SURFACE IS 33.5 MPH.

THE LARGEST RECORDED FRUIT CROP YIELD IS FROM THE WATERMELON, WITH 350 POUNDS FROM A SINGLE PLANT.

MOST OF THE VISIBLE STARS YOU SEE IN THE NIGHT SKY ARE TWO STARS ORBITING EACH OTHER.

A binary star or binary star system is a system of two stars that are gravitationally bound to and in orbit around each other. Binary stars in the night sky that are seen as a single object to the naked eye are often resolved using a telescope as separate stars, in which case they are called visual binaries.

BOTH VOLLEYBALL AND BASKETBALL WERE INVENTED IN MASSACHUSETTS.

"THE CURE FOR INSOMNIA" IS THE LONGEST MOVIE EVER, RUNNING FOR 85 HOURS.

Unlike traditional movies, this experimental film was designed to cure insomnia and reprogram an insomniac's biological clock.

VOLVO INVENTED THE THREE-POINT SEAT BELT AND THEN GAVE FREE LICENSES TO ALL OTHER AUTO MANUFACTURERS TO USE IT.

THE FIRST CAN OPENER WASN'T INVENTED UNTIL ALMOST 50 YEARS AFTER THE INVENTION OF THE CAN.

RIPE CRANBERRIES WILL
BOUNCE
LIKE RUBBER BALLS.

Cranberries are commonly referred to as "bounce berries" because they bounce when they're ripe. In fact, bouncing cranberries is a common ripeness test for farmers and consumers alike.

THE FIRST THING EVER SOLD ON THE
INTERNET
WAS A BAG OF WEED.

In 1972, long before eBay or Amazon, students from Stanford University in California and MIT in Massachusetts conducted the first ever online transaction. Using the Arpanet account at their artificial intelligence lab, the Stanford students sold their counterparts a tiny amount of marijuana.

WHILE THE WRIGHT BROTHERS ARE FAMOUS AS A PAIR, THEY ACTUALLY ONLY FLEW TOGETHER ONCE. THEY PROMISED THEIR FATHER THEY'D ALWAYS FLY SEPARATELY.

THE WORD "TESTIFY" IS BASED ON THE ANCIENT ROMAN PRACTICE OF MAKING MEN SWEAR ON THEIR TESTICLES WHEN MAKING A STATEMENT IN COURT.

In ancient Rome, two men taking an oath of allegiance held each other's testicles, and men held their own testicles as a sign of truthfulness while bearing witness in a public forum.

IN MEDIEVAL ENGLAND, BEER WAS OFTEN SERVED WITH BREAKFAST.

Beer hasn't always been a drink of pleasure but it was drunk in greater quantities and in great variety. Some medieval beers had lower alcohol content and were drunk for breakfast. Other stronger beers were for lunch and dinner and at the end of the day.

THE OLDEST "YOUR MOM" JOKE WAS DISCOVERED ON A 3,500-YEAR-OLD BABYLONIAN TABLET.

80% OF GREECE IS MADE UP OF MOUNTAINS.

MR. BEAN HAS A MASTER'S DEGREE IN ELECTRICAL ENGINEERING.

AUSTRALIA ONCE LOST A WAR TO EMUS (THE BIRDS).

THE NEANDERTHAL'S BRAIN WAS BIGGER THAN YOURS IS.

Neanderthals had larger brains than modern humans do, and a new study of a Neanderthal child's skeleton now suggests this is because their brains spent more time growing.

THE SURFACE AREA OF THE HUMAN LUNG IS ROUGHLY THE SAME SIZE AS A TENNIS COURT.

THE "L.L." IN L.L. BEAN STANDS FOR LEON LEONWOOD.

MONTHS THAT BEGIN WITH A SUNDAY WILL ALWAYS HAVE A "FRIDAY THE 13TH."

The 13th day of the month is very slightly more likely to be a Friday than any other day of the week. Any month that starts on a Sunday contains a Friday the 13th, and there is at least one Friday the 13th in every calendar year.

A SQUARE MILE OF FERTILE EARTH HAS 32,000,000 EARTHWORMS IN IT.

VANILLA BEANS ARE THE PRODUCT OF THE WORLD'S ONLY FRUIT-PRODUCING ORCHID, THE VANILLA PLANIFOLIA.

THE KATYDID BUG HEARS THROUGH HOLES IN ITS HIND LEGS.

HORSES ARE DISTANT RELATIVES OF RHINOCEROSES.

Despite looking almost nothing alike, we've known that rhinos, horses and tapirs are cousins since the 19th century. According to the American Museum of Natural History, "Horses belong to a group of mammals with an odd number of toes (yes they have toes)." Most members of this group, known as perissodactyla, are extinct but some species survived. They include rhinoceroses and tapirs, the horse's closest living relatives.

NON-DAIRY
CREAMER
IS FLAMMABLE.

Non-dairy powdered creamer is flammable because it is a powder and has a high surface area to oxygen ratio. This means that it is easy to ignite and flames can spread quickly.

THE COUPLE IN THE PAINTING "AMERICAN GOTHIC" ARE ACTUALLY FATHER AND DAUGHTER AND NOT HUSBAND AND WIFE.

QUEEN ELIZABETH I OF ENGLAND, USING A DIAMOND, SCRATCHED THE FOLLOWING MESSAGE ON HER PRISON WINDOW: "MUCH SUSPECTED OF ME, NOTHING PROVED CAN BE."

YOUR BODY HAS ENOUGH IRON IN IT TO MAKE A METAL NAIL 3 INCHES LONG.

IN FRANCE, WOMEN COULD TAKE THEIR HUSBANDS TO COURT FOR IMPOTENCE.

In 16th century France, men who were not able to please their wives in bed were summoned before the Court. This is because one of the few reasons the Church would allow a woman a divorce was if her husband could not perform sexually to meet her expectations.

BUBBLE GUM CONTAINS RUBBER.

THE HUMAN EYE CAN DISTINGUISH ABOUT 10 MILLION DIFFERENT COLORS.

AT ANY ONE TIME ABOUT 0.7% OF THE WORLD'S POPULATION IS DRUNK.

DOGS HAVE BEEN BANNED FROM ANTARCTICA.

The last dogs were taken from Antarctica on Feb 22nd 1994, a consequence of an environmental clause in the Antarctic Treaty that required non-native species to be removed. In the case of dogs, this was specifically because distemper (a disease of dogs) could potentially spread from the dogs to the native seals of Antarctica.

THE HUMAN HEART PUMPS 1.5 MILLION BARRELS OF BLOOD DURING AN AVERAGE LIFETIME, ENOUGH TO FILL 200 TRAIN TANK CARS.

RATS MULTIPLY SO QUICKLY THAT IN 18 MONTHS, TWO RATS COULD HAVE OVER A MILLION DESCENDANTS.

BABY ROBINS EAT 14 FEET OF EARTHWORMS EVERY DAY.

By five days of age, the nestlings get earthworms that parents break into small mouthfuls. Each young robin may eat 14 feet of earthworms in a two-week nest life—and worms are not even their main food!

A GOAT SERVED AS A LANCE CORPORAL IN THE BRITISH ARMY.

William "Billy" Windsor I is a cashmere goat who served as a lance corporal in the 1st Battalion, the Royal Welsh, an infantry battalion of the British Army. He served as a lance corporal from 2001 until 2009, except for a three-month period in 2006 when he was demoted to fusilier, after inappropriate behaviour during the Queen's Official Birthday celebrations while deployed on active duty with the battalion on Cyprus. He retired to Whipsnade Zoo in May 2009.

SOFT-SHELLED TURTLES
URINATE
THROUGH THEIR MOUTH.

A team of biologists has published a paper revealing that when Chinese soft-shelled turtles mysteriously dunk their heads in puddles for up to 100 minutes at a time, they are in fact urinating from their mouths. More specifically, they're excreting most of their urea this way.

THE EARTH

USED

TO BE PURPLE.

The earliest life on Earth might have been just as purple as it is green today, a scientist claims. Ancient microbes might have used a molecule other than chlorophyll to harness the Sun's rays, one that gave the organisms a violet hue.

THE MODERN OLYMPIC GAMES WERE FIRST HELD IN 1896 IN ATHENS, GREECE, WITH 14 NATIONS PARTICIPATING.

THE MOST EXPENSIVE PIZZA IN THE WORLD COSTS OVER $12,000 AND TAKES 72 HOURS TO MAKE.

The most expensive pizza in the world is known as the "Louis XIII" and is made by Chef Renato Viola in Salerno, Italy. This pizza is topped with a variety of rare and expensive ingredients, including three types of caviar, lobster from Norway, and bufala mozzarella. It is also garnished with pink Australian sea salt and 24-carat gold leaf.

THE ONLY 15 LETTER WORD THAT CAN BE SPELLED WITHOUT REPEATING A LETTER IS UNCOPYRIGHTABLE.

THE PHRASE "HANDS DOWN" COMES FROM HORSE RACING.

It refers to a jockey who's so far ahead that he can afford to drop his hands and loosen the reins (usually kept tight to encourage a horse to run) and still easily win.

ISAAC ASIMOV IS THE ONLY AUTHOR TO HAVE A BOOK IN EVERY DEWEY-DECIMAL CATEGORY.

IT'S AGAINST THE LAW TO BURP OR SNEEZE IN CERTAIN CHURCHES IN OMAHA, NEBRASKA.

IN MOST ADVERTISEMENTS, INCLUDING NEWSPAPERS, THE TIME DISPLAYED ON A WATCH IS 10:10.

THE CHANCES OF MAKING TWO HOLES-IN-ONE IN A ROUND OF GOLF ARE ONE IN 67 MILLION.

SOME SPECIES OF FROGS AND TOADS USE PRESSURE FROM THEIR EYEBALLS TO HELP SWALLOW THEIR FOOD.

These frogs and toads can withdraw their eyeballs inside their heads in order to help create the pressure needed to change the saliva and push the insect off the tongue and down the throat.

THE EARTH'S AGE IS ESTIMATED TO BE OVER 4.54 BILLION YEARS.

ONE OF THE VERY FIRST BICYCLES WAS CALLED THE DANDY HORSE.

The dandy horse or running machine was invented by Karl von Drais in 1818. This contraption was propelled by the rider pushing himself along with his feet on the ground. Lacking pedals, a steering mechanism and brakes, it was difficult and even dangerous to maneuver.

STEEL IS MUCH MORE ELASTIC THAN RUBBER.

Elasticity is the ability of a body to return to its previous state when an external stress and strain is applied on it. A body is said to be more elastic if it returns to its original configuration faster than others.

LIGHT SLOWS DOWN WHEN IT PASSES THROUGH WATER.

PENGUINS CAN
CONVERT
SALTWATER INTO FRESHWATER.

The supraorbital gland is a type of lateral nasal gland found in penguins, which removes sodium chloride from the bloodstream. The gland's function is similar to that of the kidneys, though it is much more efficient at removing salt, allowing penguins to survive without access to fresh water.

THE BRONTOSAURUS
NEVER
EXISTED.

Brontosaurus, whose name means "Thunder Lizard," is not an actual dinosaur. It is actually a mix of Apatosaurus, meaning "Deceptive Lizard," and Camarasaurus, meaning "Chambered Lizard."

THERE ARE OVER 9,000 BENCHES IN CENTRAL PARK.

THE VERY FIRST BOMB DROPPED BY THE ALLIES ON BERLIN DURING WORLD WAR II KILLED SEVEN ELEPHANTS IN THE BERLIN ZOO.

THE SANSKRIT WORD FOR "WAR" MEANS "DESIRE FOR MORE COWS."

THE PRAYING MANTIS IS THE ONLY INSECT THAT CAN TURN ITS HEAD.

Between the head and the thorax there is a flexible joint that allows mantises to swivel their heads around 180 degrees, the only insect that can do so.

SPOTTED SKUNKS DO HANDSTANDS BEFORE THEY SPRAY.

Like all skunks, spotted skunks produce a nasty-smelling spray to deter predators. However, spotted skunks also do a flashy handstand on their front legs as an extra warning before they spray.

THERE ARE MORE CHICKENS THAN PEOPLE IN THE WORLD.

SLUGS HAVE 4 NOSES.

THE MAIN LIBRARY AT INDIANA UNIVERSITY SINKS OVER AN INCH EVERY YEAR BECAUSE WHEN IT WAS BUILT, ENGINEERS FAILED TO TAKE INTO ACCOUNT THE WEIGHT OF ALL THE BOOKS THAT WOULD OCCUPY THE BUILDING.

THE WORD "CHECKMATE" IN CHESS COMES FROM THE PERSIAN PHRASE "SHAH MAT," WHICH MEANS "THE KING IS DEAD."

SIGMUND FREUD HAD A MORBID FEAR OF FERNS.

Sigmund Freud reportedly suffered from pteridophobia, a morbid fear of ferns. This is a subset of a more extensive fear of all plants, known as botanophobia.

RECYCLING ONE GLASS JAR SAVES ENOUGH ENERGY TO WATCH T.V. FOR THREE HOURS.

THE AVERAGE BANK TELLER LOSES ABOUT $250 EVERY YEAR.

THE HIGHEST POINT IN PENNSYLVANIA IS LOWER THAN THE LOWEST POINT IN COLORADO.

Mt. Davis is the highest point in Pennsylvania, at an elevation of 3,213 feet, and the lowest point in Colorado is the Arkansas river, which is 3,315 feet above sea level.

THROWING SPICES AT A SINGLE PERSON IS A TRADITION IN DENMARK.

In Denmark, if you're still single when you turn 25, you're going to get covered in cinnamon. The tradition dates back hundreds of years to when spice salesmen would stay bachelors because they traveled so much.

ABRAHAM LINCOLN FED
HIS CAT
WITH A GOLD FORK.

*Lincoln's affection for cats was so profound that he even served them at the
table during a formal dinner at the White House. Upon his wife's remark
that such behavior was "shameful" in the presence of their guests, he retorted,
"If a gold fork was suitable for ex-President James Buchanan,
then it's certainly suitable for Tabby."*

"BOOKKEEPER" AND "BOOKKEEPING" ARE THE ONLY UNHYPHENATED ENGLISH WORDS WITH THREE CONSECUTIVE DOUBLE LETTERS.

FIRE HOUSES WERE EQUIPPED WITH SPIRAL STAIRCASES SO HORSES WOULD NOT TRY TO CLIMB THE STAIRS INTO THE LIVING QUARTERS.

THE INTERNATIONAL TELEPHONE DIALING CODE FOR ANTARCTICA IS 672.

THE NATIONAL ANTHEM OF GREECE HAS 158 VERSES. NO ONE IN GREECE HAS MEMORIZED ALL 158 VERSES.

BEFORE THE ERASER, BREAD WAS USED TO REMOVE PENCIL MARKS.

Until the 1770s, humanity's preferred way of erasing errant graphite marks relied on bread that had been de-crusted, moistened and balled up.

THE PLACEMENT OF A DONKEY'S EYES IN ITS HEAD ENABLES IT TO SEE ALL FOUR FEET AT ALL TIMES.

THERE WASN'T A SINGLE PONY IN THE PONY EXPRESS, JUST HORSES.

NUTMEG IS EXTREMELY POISONOUS IF INJECTED INTRAVENOUSLY.

SYLVIA MILES HAD THE SHORTEST PERFORMANCE EVER NOMINATED FOR AN OSCAR WITH "MIDNIGHT COWBOY." HER ENTIRE ROLE LASTED ONLY SIX MINUTES.

THE MICROWAVE WAS INVENTED AFTER A RESEARCHER WALKED BY A RADAR TUBE AND A CHOCOLATE BAR MELTED IN HIS POCKET.

In 1945 engineer Percy Spencer was researching radar at the Raytheon company. He stopped for a minute in front of a magnetron, an electronic vacuum tube that generates high-frequency radio waves. Suddenly feeling a strange sensation, he noticed that the chocolate bar in his pocket was melting.

THE STATE OF FLORIDA IS BIGGER THAN ENGLAND.

THE NAME JEEP CAME FROM THE ABBREVIATION USED IN THE ARMY FOR THE "GENERAL PURPOSE" VEHICLE, G.P.

THE WORD "SAMBA" MEANS "TO RUB NAVELS TOGETHER."

MEL BLANC (THE VOICE OF BUGS BUNNY) WAS ALLERGIC TO CARROTS.

IN 1984, A CANADIAN FARMER BEGAN RENTING AD SPACE ON HIS COWS.

JOHN LENNON'S FIRST GIRLFRIEND WAS NAMED THELMA PICKLES.

THE WORLD'S OLDEST PIECE OF
CHEWING
GUM IS 9,000 YEARS OLD.

The oldest known example of birch-pitch chewing gum dates back an impressive 9,880–9,540 years and was discovered in western Sweden.

HONEY
NEVER
SPOILS.

In 2015, archaeologists reported that they'd found 3,000-year-old honey while excavating tombs in Egypt, and it was perfectly edible.

THE PHRASE "RULE OF THUMB" IS DERIVED FROM AN OLD ENGLISH LAW WHICH STATED THAT YOU COULDN'T BEAT YOUR WIFE WITH ANYTHING WIDER THAN YOUR THUMB.

THE EISENHOWER INTERSTATE SYSTEM REQUIRES THAT ONE MILE IN EVERY FIVE MUST BE STRAIGHT.

Early regulations required that one out of every five miles of the Interstate Highway System must be built straight and flat, so as to be usable by aircraft during times of war.

LEE HARVEY OSWALD'S CADAVER TAG SOLD AT AN AUCTION FOR $6,600 IN 1992.

IT WAS ONCE AGAINST THE LAW TO SLAM YOUR CAR DOOR IN A CITY IN SWITZERLAND.

Technically speaking, it is still against the law to slam your door, as the law forbids making "unnecessarily loud and disruptive noise" between the hours of 11pm and 6am.

THERE ARE MORE THAN 4,000 TRADITIONAL DANCES IN GREECE.

Greece's diverse traditional dances encompass a wide array of styles, from the lively Sirtaki to the intricate Tsamiko. Rooted in history, mythology, and regional customs, these dances serve as vibrant expressions of Greek identity and cultural pride.

IN ENGLAND, IN THE 1880'S, "PANTS" WAS CONSIDERED A DIRTY WORD.

IT'S AGAINST THE LAW TO CATCH FISH WITH YOUR BARE HANDS IN KANSAS.

UNTIL 1796, THERE WAS A STATE IN THE UNITED STATES CALLED FRANKLIN.

Today it is known as Tennessee. The State of Franklin was an autonomous, secessionist United States territory that was created shortly after the American Revolution. This territory was later ceded by North Carolina to the federal government and became part of the state of Tennessee.

IN BANGLADESH, KIDS AS YOUNG AS 15 CAN BE JAILED FOR CHEATING ON THEIR FINALS.

IT TAKES A LOBSTER APPROXIMATELY SEVEN YEARS TO GROW TO BE ONE POUND.

GERMANY HAS MORE CASTLES THAN THERE ARE MCDONALD'S IN THE UNITED STATES.

Germany is estimated to have 25,000 castles, and there are around 13,000 McDonald's locations in America.

DOGS ARE ONE OF THE THREE DEADLIEST ANIMALS IN THE UK. THE OTHER TWO ARE BEES AND COWS.

MOST HAMSTERS ONLY

BLINK

ONE EYE AT A TIME.

Hamsters blink their eyes to clean them of any foreign particles such as dust. However, unlike human beings, they blink their eyes independently of each other. They only blink one eye at a time to stay alert for predators.